3-10

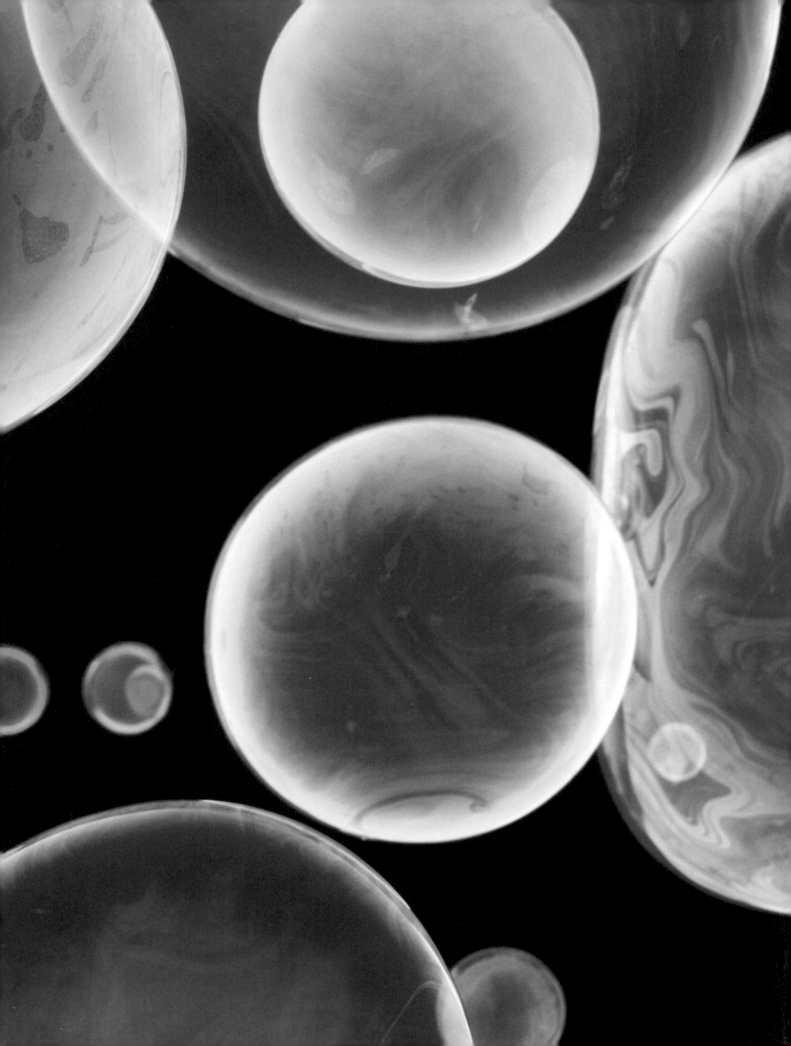

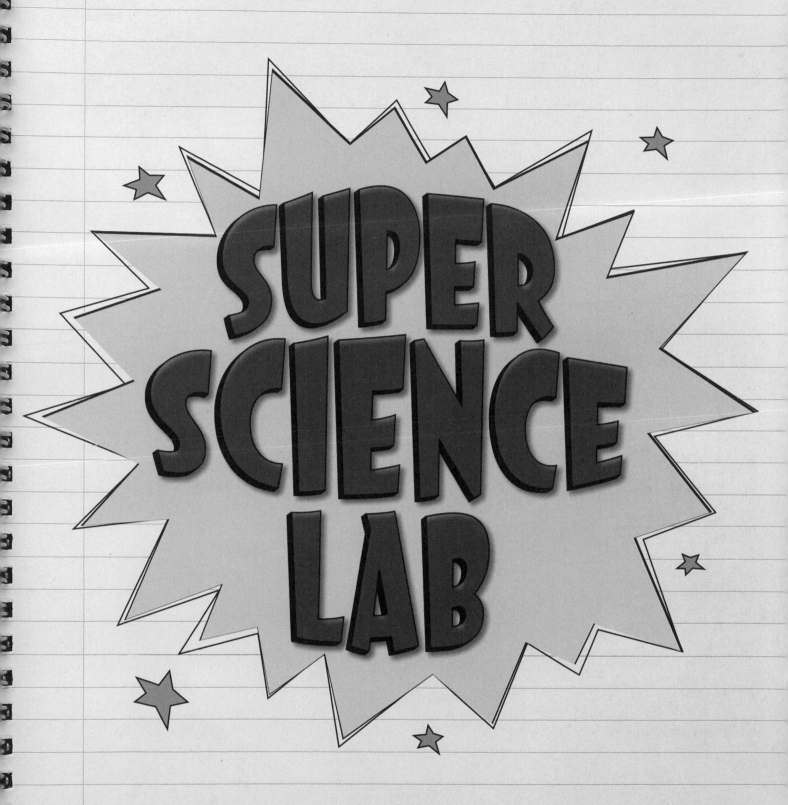

SUPER SCIENCE LAB

DK Publishing

DK

LONDON, NEW YORK, MELBOURNE, MUNICH, AND DELHI

Editors Joe Harris, Wendy Horobin, Ben Morgan, Penny Smith
Project Designers Sadie Thomas, Jess Bentall
Designers Gemma Fletcher, Hedi Hunter,
Lauren Rosier, Laura Roberts-Jensen
Science Consultant Francis Bate
Photography Andy Crawford, Guy Archard
Illustrations Laurie Peters
Picture Researcher Rob Nunn
Indexer Chris Bernstein
Production Editor Sean Daly
Jacket Designers Jess Bentall, Natalie Godwin
Jacket Editor Mariza O'Keeffe
US Editor Margaret Parrish
Publishing Manager Bridget Giles
Art Director Rachael Foster
Creative Director Jane Bull
Category Publisher Mary Ling

First published in the United States in 2009 by
DK Publishing
375 Hudson Street, New York, New York 10014

A September Films Production in association with
Hamster's Wheel Productions as seen on BBC.

Text © 2009 Richard Hammond & September Films Limited
Layout and design © 2009 Dorling Kindersley Limited
09 10 11 12 13 10 9 8 7 6 5 4 3 2 1
RD184 – 01/09

The catalog record for this book is available
from the Library of Congress.

ISBN: 978-0-7566-5341-5

Color reproduction by Alta Image, UK
Printed and bound by L. Rex, China

Discover more at
www.dk.com

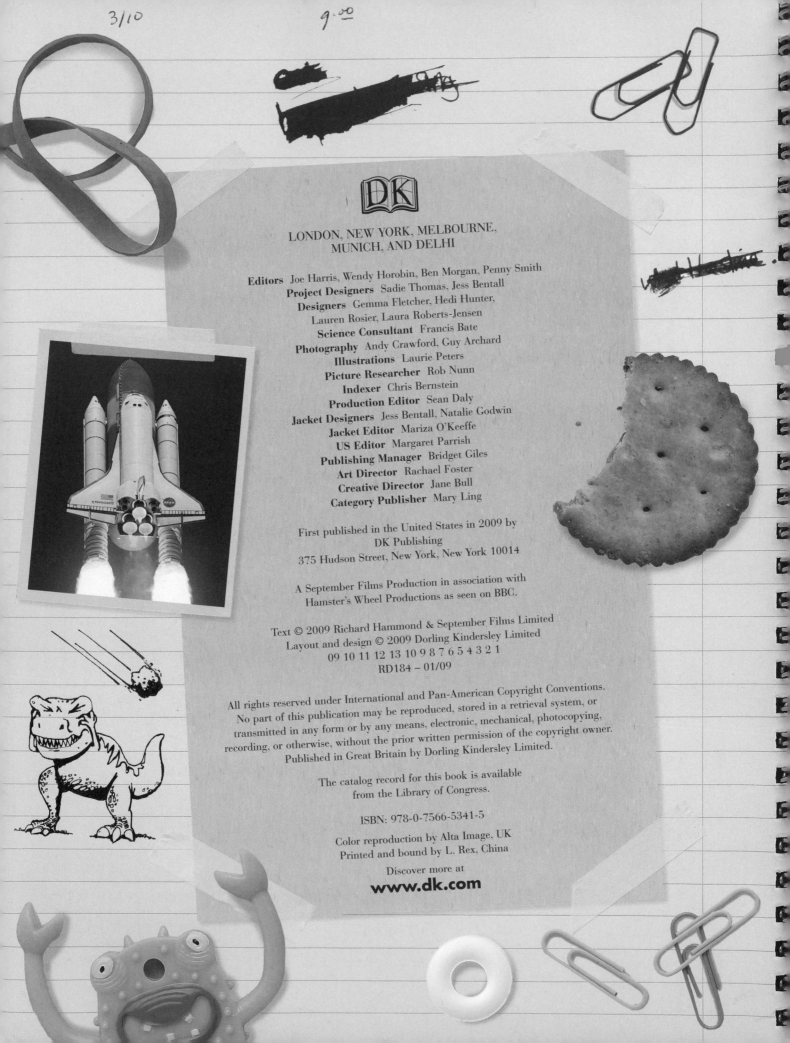

Introduction

Ever wondered what happens when you zap a bar of soap in the microwave or drop mints into a cola bottle? Want to know **how to make slime**, turn a glass of water upside down without it spilling, or stab a balloon WITHOUT bursting it? If you have, you've come to the right place. And if you haven't, you've also come to the right place, because THESE ACTIVITIES ARE 100% GUARANTEED TO BLOW YOU AWAY.

I love all things scientific and mechanical, from bikes and cars to Isaac Newton's rather cunning laws of motion. And with a bit of help from one or two experts, I've had GREAT FUN conducting fascinating and, erm, extremely important scientific research for this book.

You may have heard people on TV saying, "Please don't try this at home." Well, you won't find those words anywhere in these pages. **You could say the motto for this book is "Please DO try this at home,"** because this book is PACKED FULL OF ACTIVITIES that anyone can try anywhere. And they're all about the weird and wonderful side of science: the shocking, the bizarre, the impossible, and the downright disgusting. **It's science, but not as you know it.**

And it's all 100% safe and fine for you to do at home. Well, pretty much. Just make sure you stand back far enough...

RICHARD HAMMOND

Contents

It's easy to perform **experiments** with odds and ends from around your home.

Do you know how to make **slime balls**?

Science can be really revolting.

How can mints cause an eruption?

↑↑↑

"Make sure you keep your notebook neat and clean." Yeah, right!

UP, UP, AND AWAY

Meet the real-life Buzz Lightyear. In September 2008, daredevil Swiss inventor Yves Rossy **strapped a jet-powered wing** on his back and soared across the English Channel. In this section you can **defy gravity** yourself and find out more about things that float or fly, from rockets and bubbles to paper planes and table-tennis balls (yes, really).

Bottle rocket

Prepare for blastoff! This simple rocket won't go quite as far as the MOON, but it should be able to clear the **roof of your house.** You'll need an adult to help with this experiment.

Why not decorate your rocket?

HELP!

1. **Take the lid off** a sports drink bottle. Fill the bottle about a third full with WATER, then put the lid back on. **Pull the bottle cap open** and firmly push the foot-pump nozzle into it.

2. **If the nozzle is blocked** by plastic in the cap, get an adult to poke the plastic out with a pair of scissors.

   *If the nozzle **doesn't fit** tightly enough, wrap tape around it.*

3. **Turn three flowerpots** upside down, and arrange them in a TRIANGLE. Turn the bottle upside down, and rest it between the flowerpots so it is pointing at the **sky**, but away from you.

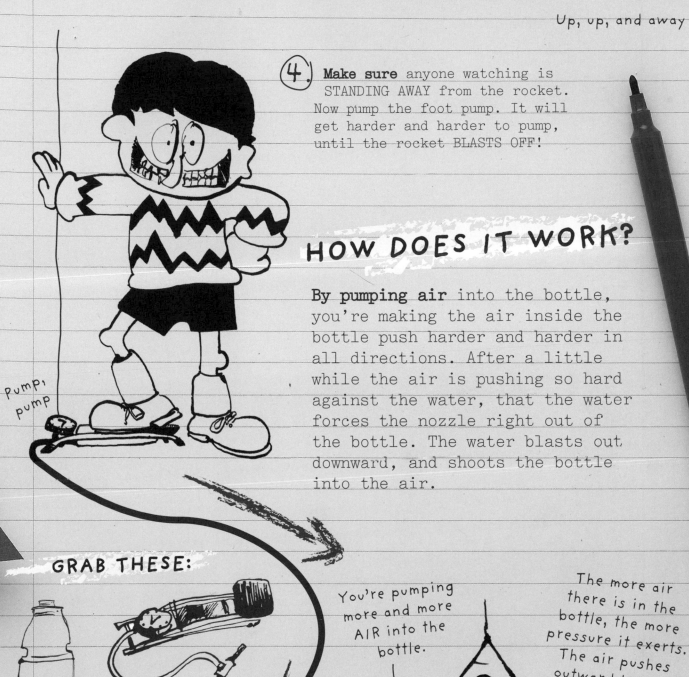

4. **Make sure** anyone watching is STANDING AWAY from the rocket. Now pump the foot pump. It will get harder and harder to pump, until the rocket BLASTS OFF!

Pump, pump

HOW DOES IT WORK?

By pumping air into the bottle, you're making the air inside the bottle push harder and harder in all directions. After a little while the air is pushing so hard against the water, that the water forces the nozzle right out of the bottle. The water blasts out downward, and shoots the bottle into the air.

GRAB THESE:

An empty sports drink bottle

A foot pump with a cone-shaped nozzle

Three flowerpots

Scissors

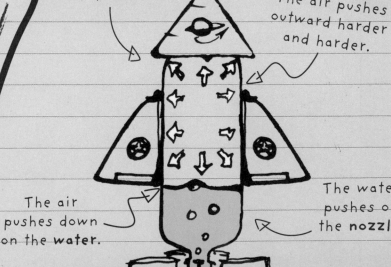

You're pumping more and more AIR into the bottle.

The more air there is in the bottle, the more pressure it exerts. The air pushes outward harder and harder.

The air pushes down on the **water**.

The water pushes on the **nozzle**.

11

Rocket science

Rockets and missiles are basically metal tubes packed with chemicals. What does it take to get them off the ground and into the air?

The answer is PHYSICS. In particular, it's the law that says that for every ACTION there is an **equal** and **opposite** reaction.

Lifting a rocket off the ground requires FORCE, and this comes from burning fuel. When fuel burns, it produces hot exhaust gases. As these **explode out** of the rocket (the action), they push the rocket in the OPPOSITE direction (the reaction). This push is called **thrust**.

WEIGHT
The weight of a rocket is the force produced by gravity pulling down on its mass.

DRAG
This force acts in the opposite direction from the rocket and is caused by air getting in the way.

THRUST
This is the powerful force that lifts the rocket off the ground.

There are THREE MAIN FORCES acting on a rocket: WEIGHT, THRUST, and DRAG. Rockets are usually tall and thin to minimize losses from drag, which slows the rocket down.

ROCKET FACTS

At launch, a **space shuttle** and its rockets weigh a total of 4½ MILLION lb (2 million kg). That's as heavy as 500 elephants. To get off the ground, each of the two **booster rockets** and three **shuttle engines** must produce enough thrust to overcome the shuttle's weight. The force they produce PUSHES the shuttle upward at an average speed of **6,000 mph** (9,500 km/h).

A rocket on the Moon weighs a sixth of what it does on Earth...

... because there is less **gravity** on the Moon. As a result, the rocket will need less thrust to take off.

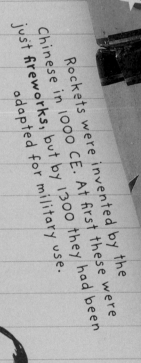

Rockets were invented by the Chinese in 1000 CE. At first these were just **fireworks**, but by 1300 they had been adapted for military use.

Steam-powered rockets were too heavy to get off the ground, but scientists discovered they worked well under water—as **torpedoes**.

Where did HE come from?

13

Bubble-o-matic

People have been blowing bubbles for hundreds of years. The first bubble toys were CLAY PIPES. Now you can find bubble guns and hoops of all shapes and sizes. But here's a brand new way to have bubbly fun: with a machine that creates a **whole cloud of bubbles.**

HOW DOES IT WORK?

As they spin around, the paperclip loops get a thin film of bubble solution stretched across them. A puff of air from the fan or hair dryer makes the film stretch, trapping air inside it. The film tightens around the air until it becomes a sphere.

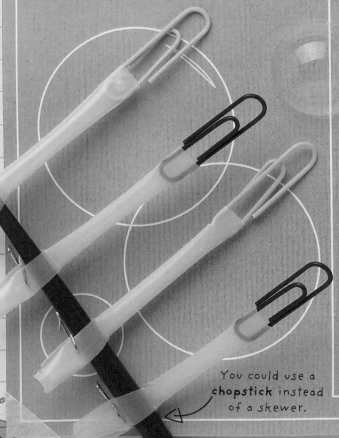

You could use a **chopstick** instead of a skewer.

1. **Take four straws,** and cut them into pieces about 2½ in (6 cm) long.

2. **Make two small snips** at one end of a piece of straw. Then slide it on to the skewer firmly, and staple it tightly in place. Make sure it can't easily spin around the stick.

3. **Push a paper clip** into the other end of the straw, making sure that two loops of the clip are showing.

4. **Now repeat this** with the other pieces of straw. Twist them around the stick at different angles.

5. **Make enough bubble mix** to fill your bowl. For each cup of water, add 2 tablespoons of dishwashing liquid. (A teaspoon of glycerin will make the bubbles stronger.)

6. **Rest** the ends of the skewer on the sides of the bowl and **spin it around** a few times. Point the hair dryer or fan at the bubble mix and turn it on at its lowest speed.

Spin the stick, and watch the bubbles fly.

Up, up, and away

BUILD A BUBBLE-O-MATIC

(1.) Cut

(2.) Snip, push, + staple

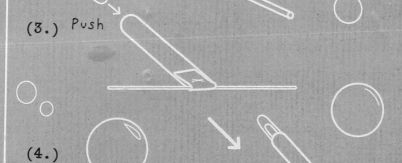

(3.) Push

(4.)

Repeat

(5.) Spin

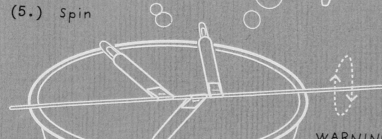

GRAB THESE:

A bowl   Paper clips

Hair dryer   Stapler
or electric fan

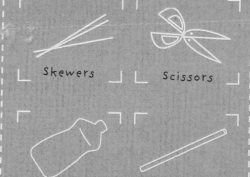

Skewers   Scissors

Dishwashing   Straws
liquid

(6.) Blow

WARNING: If you use a hair
dryer, be very careful not
to get it wet. Put it on its
coolest setting so the
bubbles don't pop.

15

The swirling colors on a bubble tell you how thick its skin is. Blue parts are thickest, then turquoise, magenta (pinkish purple), gold, and finally black. The black parts are 40 times thinner than the width of a strand of spider silk. If they get any thinner, the bubble pops.

Bubble world

When light strikes a bubble, weird things happen. Light waves **bounce back** off the outside **and** the inside of the bubble's skin, producing two sets of reflected waves that crash into each other like waves on a stormy sea. This transforms white light into fabulous, swirling bands of colored light, called **interference patterns**.

Up close, a bubble looks a bit like the planet JUPITER. It's no coincidence. Like bubbles, some planets are surrounded by a thin film of fluid (an atmosphere) that's always swirling around. In fact, some scientists study soap bubbles to figure out how storms develop on Jupiter and Earth.

Interference patterns can create colors you'd never see in a rainbow, such as magenta, silver, and gold.

Flying high

How does a **paper plane** stay in the air? Exactly the same way a real plane does. As air flows past the wings, it generates a force called LIFT that counteracts the pull of gravity.

The WIDER a plane's wings, the more lift they generate and the farther a plane can glide. But ~~paper is much too flimsy~~ for making wide wings, so paper planes tend to be **narrow** and dart-shaped. And that makes them FAST!

Folds make the paper stiffer, helping the plane to keep its shape.

TAPE a streamer to the tail of your plane and watch it flutter.

Keep the streamer as light as possible and not too long.

If you throw a paper plane **too fast,** the nose will get pushed up by the air and the plane will VEER OFF COURSE and tumble to the floor. To stop this from happening, add a paper clip or other small weight to the nose. It will help the plane fly faster.

The deep central fold is the plane's "fuselage." It helps keep the plane flat, preventing it from tilting to the left or right.

If the the nose gets crumpled in a crash, the plane won't fly properly. You can protect the nose by folding it back on itself.

Planes with narrow, stubby wings fly fastest.

Anything that flies has to overcome a force called DRAG, which is caused by air molecules **getting in the way.** To make drag as small as possible, planes or other flying objects have a narrow, streamlined shape and a **pointed** front end.

Paper planes don't have to be plane-shaped. One of the best designs—the "hoopster"—is made of two circular hoops of paper (one large, one small) taped to the ends of a straw.

Hover ball

Look—no hands! Here's a way you can make a ball FLOAT for minutes on end. But do you have the **skills** to take it through a midair obstacle course?

GRAB THESE:

A table-tennis ball

A pencil or ruler

A toilet-paper roll

A hair dryer

1. **Plug the hair dryer** in the socket, and put it on its coolest setting. Place the ball on top.

HOW DOES IT WORK?

The STREAM OF AIR from the hair dryer holds the ball up. But what stops the ball from falling sideways? This has to do with **air pressure**. Air with a high pressure—a **strong push**—will shove an object like a table-tennis ball into an area with a lower air pressure.

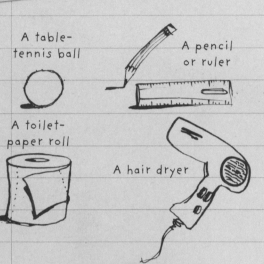

3. **Try tilting** the dryer from side to side. How far can you turn it before the ball falls?

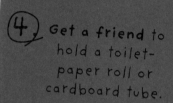

4. **Get a friend** to hold a toilet-paper roll or cardboard tube.

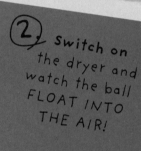

2. **Switch on** the dryer and watch the ball FLOAT INTO THE AIR!

Up, up, and away

Can you make the ball roll through it...

Can you make the ball jump over a ruler or pencil by moving the hair dryer underneath it?

(6.)

(5.) ... and catch it with the hair dryer on the other side?

PILOT OF THE YEAR

Try racing against a friend. Who'll fall first?

Slow-moving, high air pressure

Fast-moving, low air pressure

BELIEVE IT OR NOT, fast-moving air actually has a **lower pressure** than still air. So, the fast-moving air stream above the hair dryer **pushes less** on the ball than the air around it. If the ball starts to move out of the air stream, the higher pressure of the slow-moving air pushes it back to where it came from.

BRIGHT IDEAS

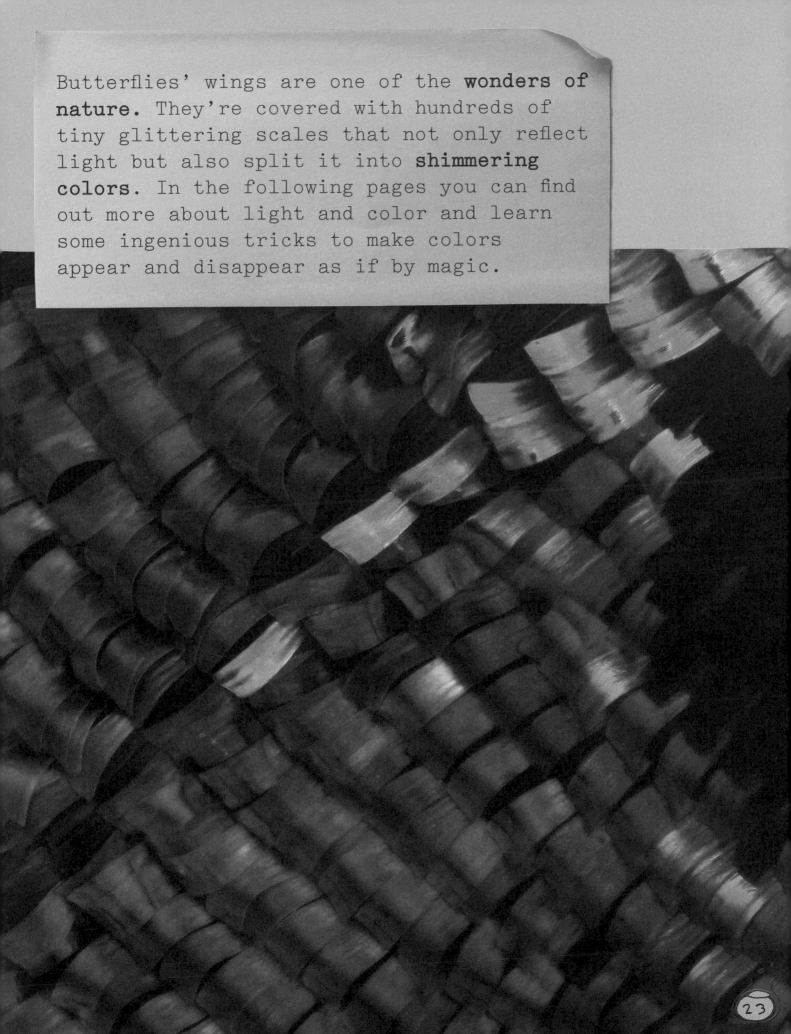

Butterflies' wings are one of the **wonders of nature.** They're covered with hundreds of tiny glittering scales that not only reflect light but also split it into **shimmering colors.** In the following pages you can find out more about light and color and learn some ingenious tricks to make colors appear and disappear as if by magic.

23

Flower power

Can't find the right color flowers for Mother's Day? Well, here's a way to solve the problem—make them CHANGE overnight simply by giving them a **drink**.

GRAB THESE:

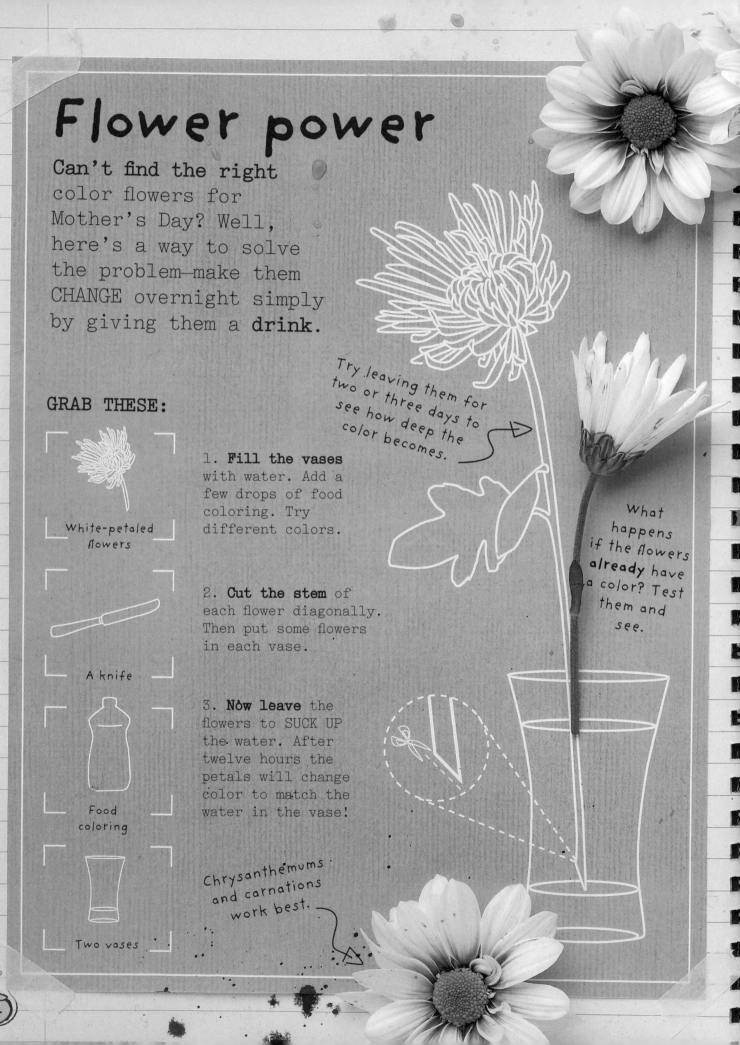

White-petaled flowers

A knife

Food coloring

Two vases

1. **Fill the vases** with water. Add a few drops of food coloring. Try different colors.

2. **Cut the stem** of each flower diagonally. Then put some flowers in each vase.

3. **Now leave** the flowers to SUCK UP the water. After twelve hours the petals will change color to match the water in the vase!

Try leaving them for two or three days to see how deep the color becomes.

What happens if the flowers **already** have a color? Test them and see.

Chrysanthemums and carnations work best.

YOU CAN EVEN MAKE A FLOWER TURN TWO DIFFERENT COLORS!

When you SPLIT the stem, the two halves of the stem each take up a different color. This will make **half** the flower one color, and the other half **another**.

As water moves UP the stem it takes the food coloring with it.

INSIDE the plant stem are tubes called **xylem tubes**. These vessels allow water and nutrients to move from the roots to the flowers.

MAKE TWO-COLOR FLOWERS

1. **Use a knife** to cut lengthwise down a flower stem, splitting it in two. Make sure that the split goes only **halfway** up.

2. **Dip each half** of the stem in a vase of different-colored water. When you come back later, you'll have a funky two-color flower!

Cabbage magic

Why is boiled cabbage like a chameleon? Because they can both CHANGE COLOR. The liquid from red cabbage is usually purple, but it can turn pink, blue, or even green.

GRAB THESE:

 Some glasses

 Half a red cabbage

A kettle

 Vinegar

A teaspoon

A knife

A pitcher

A strainer

Baking soda

Be careful with sharp knives.

1. **Chop** half a red cabbage into small pieces.

2. **Ask an adult to pour boiling water** into a pitcher with the cabbage. Leave it to cool for 10 minutes.

3. **Pour the cabbage water** through a strainer. Dilute it with cold water until it's purple but transparent.

You could also try adding: LEMON JUICE, SODA WATER, or

HOW DOES IT WORK?

Red cabbage water changes color when it's mixed with **acids** or **bases**. Acids (like vinegar) turn it PINK, but bases (like baking soda) turn it BLUE or GREEN.

Deep purple

④ **Now pour your potion** into glasses. Add some white vinegar to one glass, drop by drop. **Mix** a teaspoon of baking soda into another glass. What happens?

⑤ **How many colors** can you make by adding different amounts of each ingredient?

Bright blue

Shocking pink

LAUNDRY DETERGENT. Which are acids? Which are bases?

whizz, bang, flash!

Ever seen a **blue firework**? You won't have.
Although fireworks create a dazzling range
of colors, none produces pure blue light.
The colors come from metal elements in the
chemical mix. Strontium creates red light,
barium creates green, and sodium produces
yellow. Aluminum and magnesium blaze out
a **blinding white light.**

Each streak of light comes from what firework-makers call a "star"—a pea-sized nugget of light-emitting chemicals that glow when they get superhot.

Shine a light

Ever thought what life was like before the invention of the LIGHT BULB? It was rather dim and very smoky from burning candles and gas lamps. Then, in 1879, Joseph Swan and Thomas Edison both had the same **bright idea**...

What can I invent today?

A filament is a thin coil of metal that glows brightly when it's heated.

Display lights are filled with gases such as neon, argon, xenon, or helium, which glow with bright colors when heated.

Each filament is 6½ ft (2 m) long. It gets so **hot** that it would catch fire in air. That's why ordinary bulbs are filled with a nonflammable gas, such as argon.

When a light is switched on, electricity begins to flow through the filament, which starts to **heat up.** This makes the electrons in the atoms in the filament jump about. As they move, they give out energy in the form of light and heat.

When it's switched on, the temperature of the filament in an ordinary 100-watt light bulb reaches 4,500°F (2,200°C). Eventually the filament begins to burn away, and the light goes POP at the end of its life.

Fluorescent bulbs work in a **different** way from ordinary light bulbs. Instead of heating up a glowing filament, they use electricity to make a gas GLOW inside a coiled tube.

Most light bulbs burn for about 900 hours. Fluorescent bulbs last up to 20 times longer.

The ultraviolet light produced by the gas inside the bulb is invisible, but the coating of the bulb turns it into visible light.

The two metal bumps at the bottom of a bulb connect the bulb to the electricity supply.

Changing this must be scary!

The Empire State Building in New York City uses 3,194,547 light bulbs. The displays on the top floors are lit by 204 floodlights and 310 fluorescent bulbs.

Ordinary light bulbs waste energy. Only 10 percent of the electricity they use is turned into light— the rest is given off as HEAT. Fluorescent light bulbs are much less wasteful.

Milk planets

You don't need to leave your own home to go on a **cosmic** journey through OUTER SPACE. Just mix milk and dishwashing liquid, and you can create your own swirly, whirly **solar system!** Try using different colors for different planets.

HOW ON EARTH DOES IT WORK?

The molecules in liquids are always PULLING on each other, trying to stay together. This pull is called surface tension.

GRAB THESE:

Dishwashing liquid

Some milk

A cotton swab

Some jar lids

Food coloring

HOW TO DO IT

1. **Pour enough milk** into the jar lid to cover the bottom.

MARS

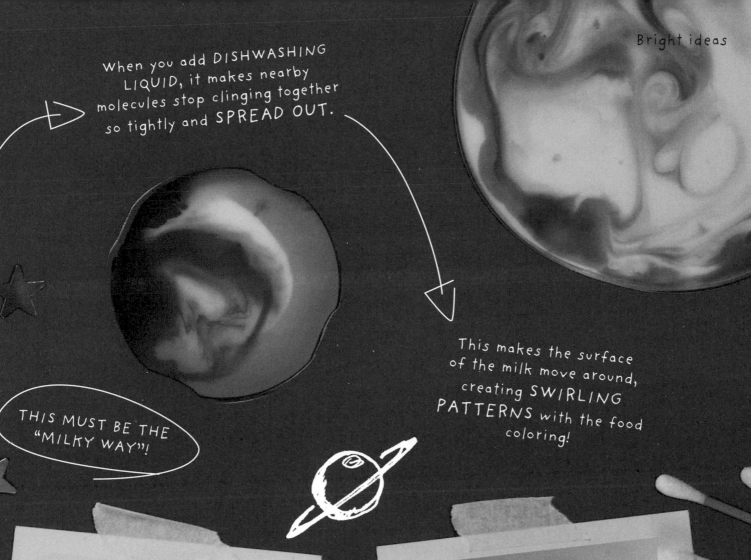

When you add DISHWASHING LIQUID, it makes nearby molecules stop clinging together so tightly and SPREAD OUT.

This makes the surface of the milk move around, creating SWIRLING PATTERNS with the food coloring!

THIS MUST BE THE "MILKY WAY"!

2. **Add some little drops** of food coloring to the milk. Use several different colors.

3. **Dip a cotton swab** in dishwashing liquid, and touch it to the milk. The colors will start to whirl around!

33

READ ALL ABOUT IT! READ ALL ABOUT IT!

ARE WE BEING INVADED? EERIE LIGHTS CAUSE PANIC

Last night, strange lights appeared in the skies above Reykjavik, Iceland. A group of tourists fled, thinking they were under attack by aliens. One witness said, "The lights looked like ghostly green curtains, with blue and red streaks. I think they were death rays."

EXCLUSIVE AWESOME AURORAS

Those green "curtains" were really an aurora. Auroras are caused by tiny particles from the Sun. Because they are charged with electricity, they are pulled toward the Earth's magnetic poles. When they collide with the atmosphere, their energy is passed to the air atoms and released as light.

HERE ARE SOME OTHER SPOOKY LIGHTS IN THE SKY

Sun dogs

Sun dogs are bright patches of light that come into view on either side of the Sun when it is low in the sky. They appear when light is reflected off **tiny ice crystals** in the atmosphere. Depending on the position of the crystals, circles (called halos) and arcs may also be formed.

Green flashes

Green flashes happen when the rays of light of a sunrise or sunset are BENT through the lower atmosphere, so that only the green part of the spectrum shows.

Ball lightning

Ball lightning is a floating, glowing ball that bounces off the ground and other objects. No one knows how it happens.

Isn't Earth a strange planet?

MAKE YOUR OWN RAINBOW

You can make your own rainbows using just a CD. Turn it over to show the shiny side, and angle it in a bright light. The CD acts like a prism and splits the light into all its different colors.

THAT'S INCREDIBLE!

Sometimes the truth is weirder than fiction. The Satanic leaf-tailed gecko of Madagascar looks so perfectly like an **old leaf** that you won't believe your eyes if you see one. This section is all about things that seem **too strange to be true,** from expanding soap monsters to boomerang cans, and other experiments that make the impossible possible.

Water stunts

Water is much stranger stuff than you may realize. Here are two ways you can surprise your friends with weird water science—by getting them SOAKING WET! If they get angry, you can say, "At least you learned some science today!"

Do this outside—grown-ups don't like wet carpets!

SNEAKY BOTTLE TRICK

GRAB THESE:

A pin   A plastic bottle

1. Fill a plastic bottle with water, and screw the lid on tightly. Use a pin to make some holes in the sides and bottom of the bottle. The water won't come out.

2. Put a sticker on the bottle that says, "DO NOT OPEN ME" and leave it for someone to find.

3. Before long, someone will be overcome with curiosity. When they **open the bottle,** the water will spray out of the holes and soak them through!

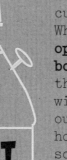

DO NOT OPEN ME

DO NOT OPEN ME

HOW DOES IT WORK?

This experiment demonstrates the invisible push of AIR PRESSURE. Gravity is always **pulling down** on the water in the bottle, but as long as the lid is on, no water will escape because the **air pressure** outside the bottle stops the water from coming out of the holes. Also, no air can get in to replace the water. When the lid is taken off, air rushes into the bottle, and it starts to PRESS DOWN ON THE WATER—and it spills **everywhere!**

SOGGY DARE GAME

GRAB THESE:

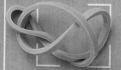 

A pin

A glass of water

A rubber band   A handkerchief

WHO'S THE BRAVEST OUT OF YOUR FRIENDS? HERE'S ONE WAY TO FIND OUT!

1. Fill a glass with water, then stretch a handkerchief over the top of it. Secure it firmly with a rubber band, so it can't move around.

2. Who dares to start the game? Hold the glass OVER THEIR HEAD, then turn it upside down. The water shouldn't spill.

An umbrella might be handy!

3. Make a few pinholes in the fabric and turn the glass upside down again. Each player then has to take turns enlarging the holes and holding it over their heads until somebody gets WET.

HOW DOES IT WORK?

The force that holds the upper layer of water molecules together is called SURFACE TENSION. As long as the holes in the cloth are small enough, the water molecules will hold on to each other strongly enough to keep from spilling. But as soon as a hole is TOO BIG for the surface tension to hold the water in... SPLOSH!!

Someone's going to get soaked!

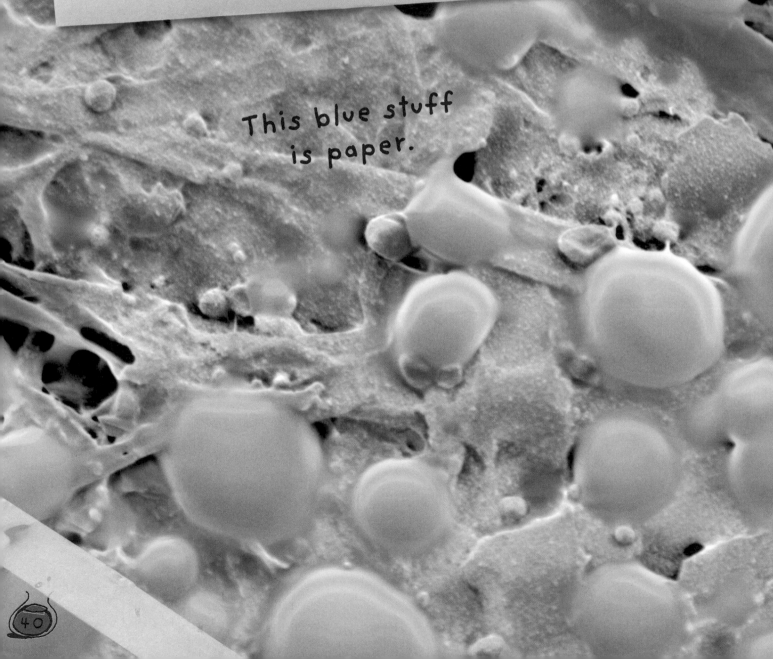

Sticking around

Under a microscope, an ordinary sticky note looks like an alien landscape. The paper is covered with **glue-filled spheres**, which burst when they're squashed. Each time you press a sticky note onto a surface, new spheres pop and **squirt out glue**—so you can stick and restick them over and over again.

This blue stuff is paper.

Boomerang can

The best experiments are like **magic tricks**—they will SURPRISE and CONFUSE your family and friends. When you roll this mysterious can along the floor, it will roll **right back** to you!

GRAB THESE:

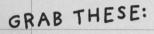
A thick rubber band

A can with a plastic lid

A small, heavy coin

Tape

3 paper clips

Scissors

(1.) Get a grown-up to do this bit.

Make a small hole in the middle of the LID of the can, and another hole in the same place on its **bottom**.

(2.)

Cut a paper clip in half, and bend it into an L shape. Tape the paper clip on to a small coin. This coin will be the weight that powers the **boomerang action**.

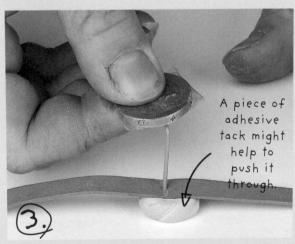
A piece of adhesive tack might help to push it through.

(3.)

Cut open the rubber band so that you have a long piece of elastic. PUSH the paper clip through the center of the rubber band. Fold the paper clip into a **U shape** to hold it in place.

42

That's incredible!

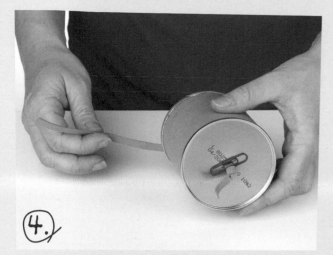

4.

Push one end of the rubber band through the bottom of the can. Make sure the coin is in the center of the can. Tie a KNOT in the end of the rubber band; thread a paper clip through the knot to **hold it in place**.

5.

Push the other end of the rubber band through the lid, and close the can. Pull the rubber band TAUT, and tie another knot. Thread a paper clip through this knot, too.

HOW DOES IT WORK?

GIVE THE CAN A PUSH...

...AND IT WILL COME BACK LIKE A BOOMERANG!

As the can ROLLS ALONG, the rubber band inside TURNS AROUND at the sides, but **stays still** in the middle, where it's held by the weight.

The rubber band gets more and more TWISTED. As it winds up, some of the energy of the rolling can is stored in the band as **potential energy**.

As soon as the can slows down, the rubber band begins to release that potential energy by **unwinding itself**. The unwinding rubber band makes the can start to roll in the **opposite** direction.

43

THE BLAST LAB BUGLE

Issue Number 476,928,053

READ ALL ABOUT IT! READ ALL ABOUT IT!

DAREDEVIL ANT SURVIVES SKYSCRAPER DEATH PLUNGE

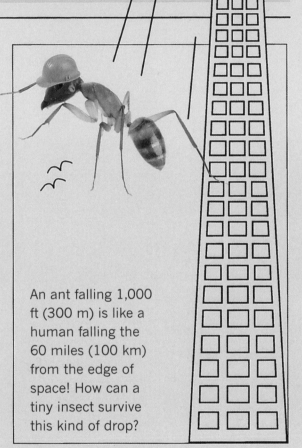

Yesterday a thrill-seeking ant fell 1,000 ft (300 m) from the top of a New York skyscraper. Heroic worker ant Antonia, 2, not only survived this death-defying drop, but did so without suffering any injury. On landing, she signed autographs for a crowd of spectators.

An ant falling 1,000 ft (300 m) is like a human falling the 60 miles (100 km) from the edge of space! How can a tiny insect survive this kind of drop?

EXCLUSIVE

WHY ANTS DON'T NEED PARACHUTES

No ant need ever be scared of heights again!

Unlike humans, ants can survive a fall from absolutely any height. How come? Any falling object reaches a maximum speed when the pull of gravity is balanced by the push of air resistance. This speed is called its terminal velocity. An ant's terminal velocity is only 5 mph (8 km/h) when it hits the ground, but a human without a parachute would be going at 125 mph (200 km/h)—SPLAT!

44

Design your own EGG parachute!

Build a tiny parachute and harness from adhesive tape, string, and a plastic bag or a hanky. Can you slow the terminal velocity enough to stop an egg from SMASHING?

That's incredible!

Whoa! Where are the brakes?

Get an adult to **drop the parachute** from an upstairs window as you watch from outside. You might want to PRACTICE first with something the same size as an egg— like a **large eraser.**

Scrambled egg anyone?

Oh dear, third time lucky!

Pump it up

Bursting a balloon is lots of fun, but do you know why it goes BANG? It has to do with pushy air molecules and rubber being **stretched** to its limit.

Around ONE hundred million air molecules are crammed inside a balloon. That's real pressure!

Push a pin in here and the balloon will BURST. That's because the rubber on the sides is STRETCHED very tightly.

POP

Stick a pin next to the **knot** and the balloon WON'T pop, because the thicker rubber at the bottom can still **stretch**.

The first balloons were made from animal bladders and intestines. Imagine blowing up one of THOSE.

If you want a really big balloon, blow one up on a foggy day. Moisture in the air helps the rubber stretch farther.

Did you know you can push a skewer **right through** a balloon without popping it? The trick is to grease it and push it through the very top and bottom of the balloon EXTREMELY GENTLY.

HELIUM balloons SHRINK faster than **air-filled** balloons. Helium atoms are extra-small and can easily squeeze through the walls of a balloon.

Let me out!

When you puncture a balloon, the rubber cracks. A split shoots around the balloon in a fraction of a second, and a blast of air rushes out in a deafening...

BANG!

A balloon's worst enemy.

Helium balloons RISE because helium is LIGHTER than air.

In 1982, American LARRY WALTERS was carried 3 miles (5 km) up into the sky by 42 HELIUM-FILLED BALLOONS tied to a garden chair. **Yikes!**

Buzz box

How steady is your hand? Find out with this fun game that will give you a real BUZZ!

GRAB THESE:

A piece of naked wire 4 in (10 cm) long

A piece of naked wire (like fuse wire) 20 in (50 cm) long

A 22 in (55 cm) flex

A shoe box

A battery with the same voltage as the buzzer

A small buzzer from an electrical store

2 flexes 8 in (20 cm) long

Tape

Ask an adult to strip the plastic from the flex.

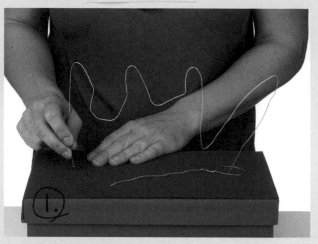

Bend the long piece of naked wire into a ZIGZAG shape. Then twist the end of the shorter piece of naked wire into a loop about the size of your thumb. Thread the loop on to the longer wire, then **stab both ends** of the zigzag through the lid of the shoebox.

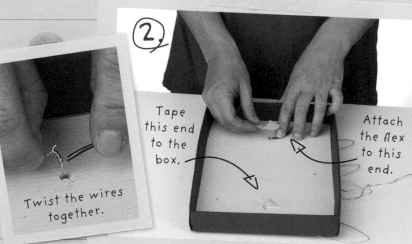

Twist the wires together.

Tape this end to the box.

Attach the flex to this end.

Tape one end of the zigzag wire to the INSIDE OF THE BOX LID. Then join the other end to one of the short pieces of flex. **Tape the join** to the box lid.

CAN YOU TAKE THE LOOP FROM ONE END OF THE ZIGZAG WIRE TO THE OTHER, WITHOUT SETTING THE BUZZER OFF? CHALLENGE YOUR FRIENDS TO SEE WHO CAN DO IT THE FASTEST!

Try using a light instead of a buzzer.

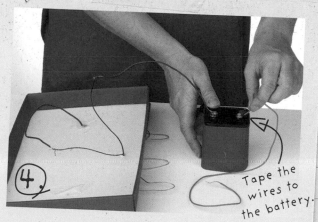

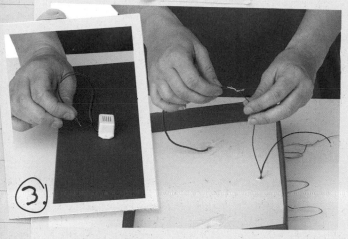

③

Make a small hole in the top of the box for the BUZZER, and push its wires through into the box. **Attach** the short piece of flex to one of the wires from the buzzer, so that the buzzer is connected to the ZIGZAG WIRE.

④

Tape the wires to the battery.

Join the buzzer to one terminal of the BATTERY with the second short flex. Connect the long flex to the **other terminal**. Put the battery in the box and thread the long flex through the lid. Join the other end of the long flex to the wire loop and tape it. **Put the lid on the box.**

HOW DOES IT WORK?

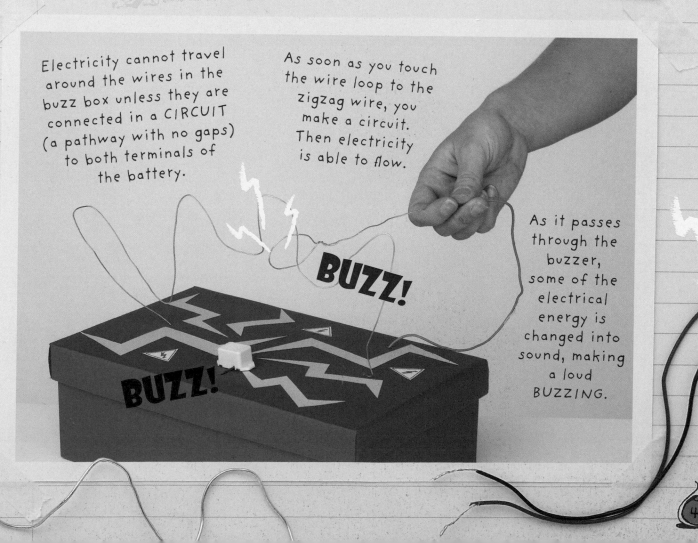

Electricity cannot travel around the wires in the buzz box unless they are connected in a CIRCUIT (a pathway with no gaps) to both terminals of the battery.

As soon as you touch the wire loop to the zigzag wire, you make a circuit. Then electricity is able to flow.

As it passes through the buzzer, some of the electrical energy is changed into sound, making a loud BUZZING.

BUZZ!

BUZZ!

Eww, GROSS!

There's a good reason why slimey, gooey, and gunky stuff is gross: it's often full of GERMS. Take sneezes, for example. The average sneeze contains 40,000 droplets of germ-laden spit and snot flying at 100 mph (160 km/h). It's the perfect way for germs to spread themselves around. This section is all about stuff that will make you go *"Eww!"* **But don't worry, it's all germ free!**

Slime time

Turn your kitchen into a toxic waste dump by mixing your own horrible, homemade **SLIME!** First follow the instructions on the right, then try **customizing** the recipe with the suggestions below.

Don't eat this mixture—it will taste horrible. Make sure you wash your hands first, or the slime could become MOLDY!

CHECK THIS OUT

* If you squeeze the slime, it feels firm...

But open your hand and it will OOZE between your fingers!

EWW!

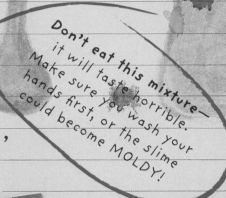

GRAB THESE:

EQUIPMENT

2 plastic cups

Spoon

Bowl

INGREDIENTS:

Water

Food coloring

Corn starch

* Try using different amounts of corn starch. How does the slime change?

* Try adding some **craft glue.** DOES IT get more sticky? More **gooey**? BOUNCIER?

* Why not try mixing a few drops of glow-in-the-dark paint into your slime?

* Or you could make slime from **outer space**, by stirring in some glitter.

Send your pals your best slime recipe.

Eww, gross!

1. **Pour a cup** of corn starch into a bowl. Slowly add water, stirring with a spoon.

2. **Keep going** until it turns gooey. You'll need about half a cup of water.

Mix

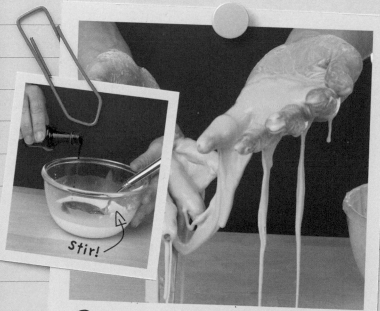

Stir!

3. **Now add a few drops** of food coloring, to make it look TOXIC.

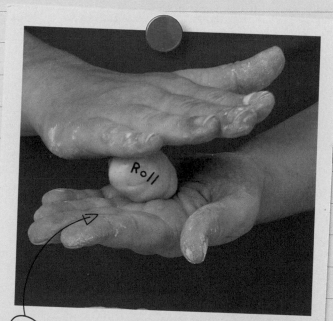

Roll

4. **Add more corn starch** and roll the slime into a ball. Squeeze it. Will it bounce?

How does it work? Turn the page to find out.

Slime science

Our slime seems to break all the rules that fluids follow—rules laid down by famous scientist Sir Isaac Newton. That's why it's called a **non-Newtonian** fluid.

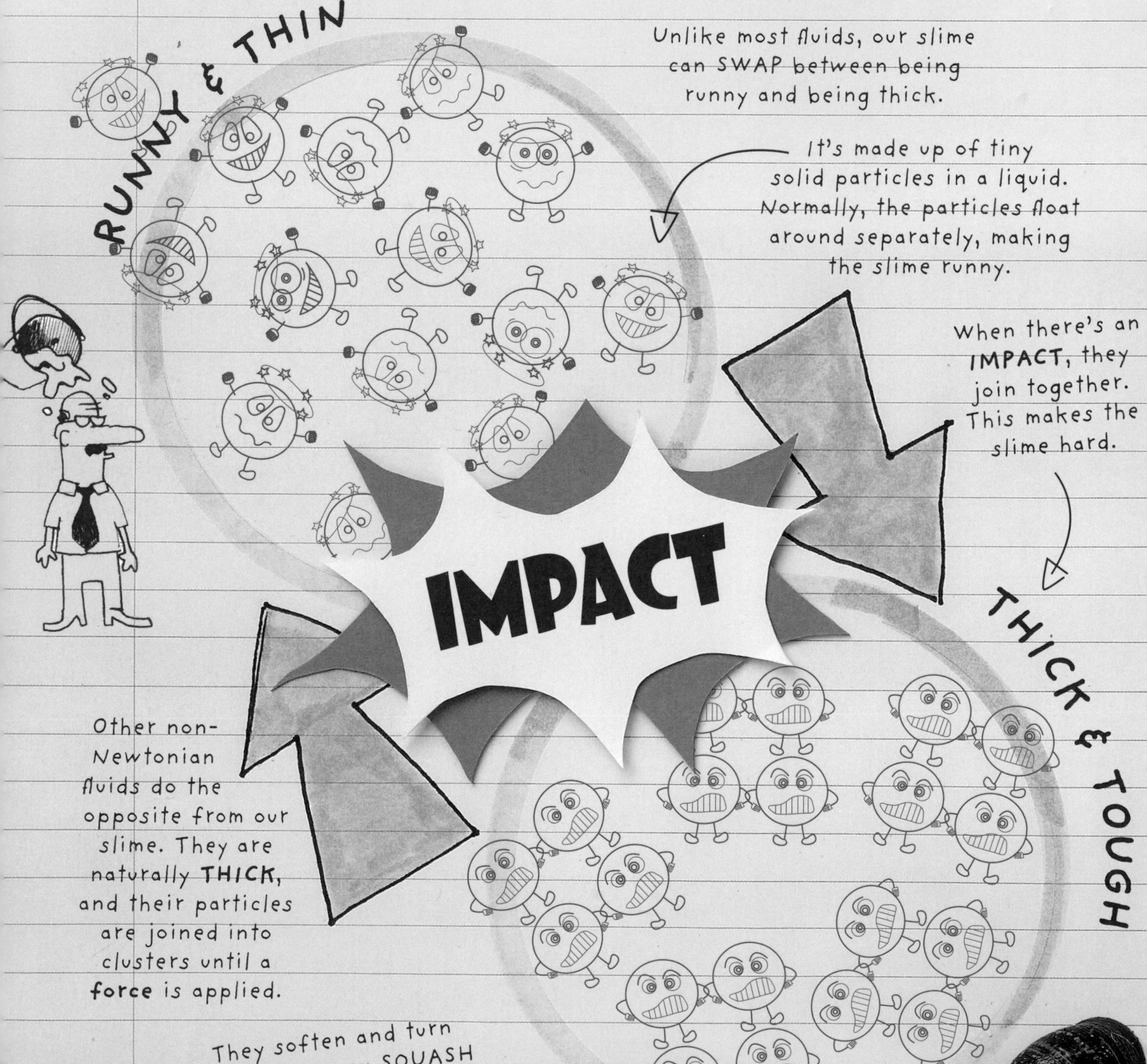

RUNNY & THIN

Unlike most fluids, our slime can SWAP between being runny and being thick.

It's made up of tiny solid particles in a liquid. Normally, the particles float around separately, making the slime runny.

When there's an **IMPACT**, they join together. This makes the slime hard.

IMPACT

THICK & TOUGH

Other non-Newtonian fluids do the opposite from our slime. They are naturally **THICK**, and their particles are joined into clusters until a **force** is applied.

They soften and turn runny when you SQUASH or SQUEEZE them.

TOUGH UNDER PRESSURE

Fluids like our slime, which get harder when they're **PUSHED** or **SQUEEZED**, have all kinds of uses.

Materials soaked in these kinds of non-Newtonian fluids are used to make protective **SPORTSWEAR** and **BODY ARMOR.** The fabric will suddenly turn HARD when something hits it.

They can be used to make **SUPERFAST SOCCER BALLS.** These harden when they're kicked.

SOGGY WHEN STRESSED

Fluids that turn **RUNNY** under pressure can also be useful... or dangerous.

Toothpaste turns liquid when you push on the tube.

The glue on the bottom of a snail's foot stays thick and **STICKY** until the snail moves. Then it becomes wet and **SLIPPERY.**

If you step into **QUICKSAND**, it acts like a sticky liquid and holds you **tight** if you struggle. But if you move slowly you should be able to crawl out.

Soap monsters

Dr. Frankenstein harnessed the power of **lightning** to create his monster. Here's how you can make some **little monsters** of your own, using the power of MICROWAVES. Did you know your bathroom was really a **monster farm?**

GRAB THESE:

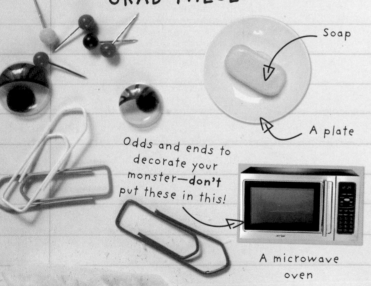

Soap

A plate

Odds and ends to decorate your monster—**don't put these in this!**

A microwave oven

DO THIS!

Place a bar of soap on a plate in the microwave. Ask an adult to put the microwave on its **highest setting,** and switch it on for about TWO minutes.

Watch the soap as it grows and changes. You can take it out when it stops growing, but give it time to **cool down** before you touch it.

Marshmallows also grow in the microwave. **BE CAREFUL—** sugar gets very hot.

GET CREATIVE

Does your soap creature look like
it has a nose, eyes, arms, or legs?
Why not decorate it?

HOW DOES IT WORK?

Microwaves make the water molecules in the soap heat up. When the water gets hot, it turns into a **gas**: water vapor. The water vapor forms bubbles, which **expand** with the heat. These bubbles make the whole bar of soap GROW.

TOP TIP

Soap that **floats** in water will work best. Try it with transparent soap as well.

"I'll lend you a hand!"

Bug ugly

For thousands of years, the SPIT of this ugly bug was more precious than gold. It's a SILKWORM—the caterpillar of a Chinese moth. Silkworms wrap themselves up in a protective ball of silk (a cocoon) when they're ready to turn into moths. The silk comes from a fine strand of spit that hardens in the air to make a tough, shiny fiber.

Silkworms have six eyes on both sides of the head, making 12 eyes altogether.

Most silkworms never grow up into moths. Once their cocoons have been made, the silk farmer drops them into boiling water to kill the silkworms. Each cocoon is then carefully unwound to make a single, mile-long thread of silk.

This is how big I really am!

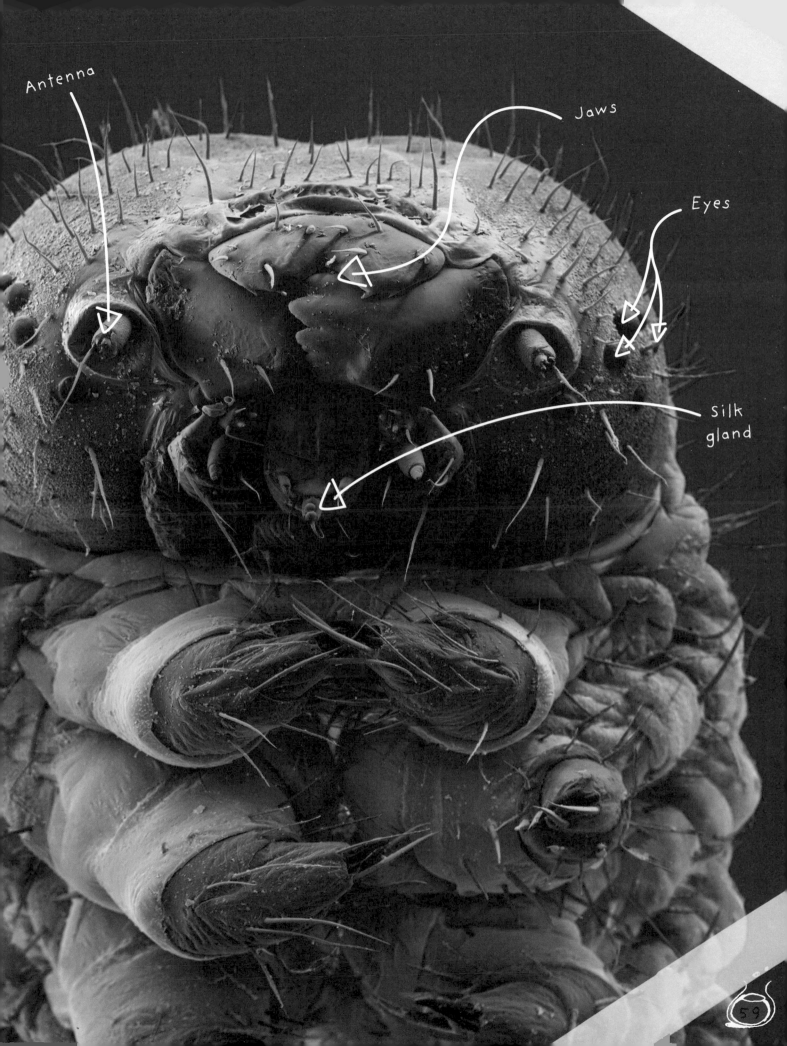

Antenna

Jaws

Eyes

Silk
gland

Gooey volcano

What happens inside a **volcano**? Find out by making your own gunge-spewing gelatin Vesuvius. This is a **sticky, messy experiment**, so make sure you protect your home from the ERUPTION.

① .

Modeling-clay plug

You could hold the funnel still with more modeling clay.

Make up some gelatin in a pitcher. Follow the instructions on the package, but only use HALF the water. Block up the funnel's hole with modeling clay, then grease the funnel with a little oil. Pour in the gelatin.

GRAB THESE:

Gelatin in different colors

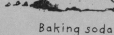
Baking soda

Food coloring

A plastic funnel

A pencil

A pitcher

A plate

A spatula

Vegetable oil

A spoon

Vinegar

A cup

A baster

A ball of modeling clay

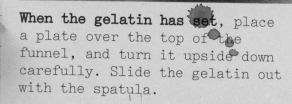

② .

When the gelatin has set, place a plate over the top of the funnel, and turn it upside down carefully. Slide the gelatin out with the spatula.

③

Use a pencil to bore a tunnel through the middle of the volcano. Stop about ¹/₂ in (1 cm) from the bottom. Use the funnel to fill the tunnel with baking soda.

④

Add a few drops of food coloring to a cup of vinegar. Suck the vinegar up into a baster. Then push it through the side of the volcano, and squeeze the vinegar into the tunnel.

Watch the volcano ERUPT!

HOW DOES IT WORK?

When you mix acids (like vinegar) and bases (like baking soda), you get a chemical reaction.

This particular acid and base reaction produces carbon dioxide gas. Bubbles of gas make the "lava" foam up out of the gelatin volcano.

PLAYING WITH
FOOD

The average watermelon is not very **stackable**—give it half a chance and it will roll around the shelf. Grow it in a box-shaped container, and your problem is solved—**square watermelon**. In this section, discover some egg-citing things you can do with food, from fizzy fountains and jelly beans to fake apple pie. **Yum.**

Jelly bean roots

Plants are not stupid. They know which way is up and which way is down. Even if you try to **confuse** them, their roots and shoots still grow in the RIGHT direction. Or do they? See if you can make a plant grow against its instincts.

Don't leave gelatin in direct sunlight—it melts!

GRAB THESE:

A package of gelatin powder

3 plastic dessert cups (one clear)

Plastic wrap

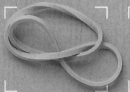

Rubber band

Bean or radish seeds

1. **Make up the gelatin powder** following the instructions on the package, using half a cup of water to $1/4$ oz (7 g) of gelatin. (Don't use fruit gelatin mix, or the experiment won't work!) Pour it into the clear cup and **leave it to set** in the fridge. While you're waiting, soak the seeds in water for two hours.

Get an adult to help you pour the hot liquid.

You could add a few drops of food coloring to the mixture.

2. **Scatter a few seeds** over the middle of the gelatin. Gently push the seeds just under the surface using the prong of a fork or a toothpick. (It's trickier to do this than you think!)

This is the bouncy part!

HOW DOES IT WORK?

Plant roots grow **downward** because their cells can detect gravity. Gravity is a force that pulls objects toward the center of Earth.

When the cup is turned **upside down**, the ROOT CELLS can still feel a downward pull and they start growing toward it.

New plant

WARNING
At the end of the experiment, throw out the gelatin. Don't eat it—nasty bacteria like it, too.

Which way does the plant shoot start growing? WHY does it do this?

3. **Cover the top of the cup** with plastic wrap. Put a **rubber band** around it to make sure it stays on. Make small holes over the seeds with a pencil so that the shoots can grow through. Put the cup on a cool windowsill away from bright sunlight or radiators.

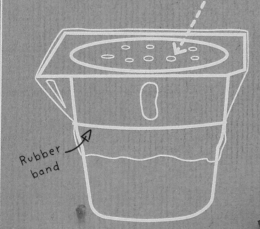

Rubber band

4. **Check the cup every day.** When the roots are about 1 in (25 mm) long, turn the cup upside down and balance the rim on the other two upturned cups.

What happens to the **roots** as the plant keeps GROWING?

Sunny side up

Eggs—we eat them for breakfast, and put them in our sandwiches and cakes. They're packed with protein and help us grow. So what's the **downside**? Well, they do come out of a chicken's backside...

BUT WHAT IS AN EGG?
A chicken's egg is a single (very big) cell. If the egg is fertilized, a chick grows inside it. But whether it's fertilized or not, the egg is pushed out of the chicken's body.

... and they're still warm when they hit the hay.

Because egg shells are porous, eggs can soak up odors from nearby foods such as smelly cheeses.

which came first, the chicken or the egg?

Inside the egg are the **white and yolk**. These are what a growing chick feeds on. The white is made of protein and water, and the yolk is rich in protein and fat. When the chick is ready to hatch, it **calls** to its mother from inside the shell.

Stand up, Mom! I'm coming out.

FRIED, BOILED, OR POACHED?
When you cook an egg you change the chemicals inside, and this makes the clear part white, and the egg hard. There's no way to change it back.

If you leave an egg to rot, **bacteria** set to work on the egg's protein. They produce hydrogen sulfide, which smells like disgustingly dirty OLD SOCKS, or, worse still, like— rotten eggs!

What are YOU looking at?

Is your egg FRESH? Put it in a bowl of water. If it sinks, it's fresh. But if it floats (because of the hydrogen sulfide gas), it's **bad**, so don't eat it!

Mostly, chickens produce eggs with one yolk, or occasionally two. However, sometimes a chicken lays an egg with **three** yolks, or with no yolks at all.

The **color** of an egg's shell has nothing to do with the egg's quality. It comes from the BREED of hen that laid the egg. Hens that lay brown eggs tend to be bigger than hens that lay white eggs.

67

A tasty trick

It's easy to fool your taste buds with the
right chemicals. This delicious apple pie
is missing an important ingredient—APPLES!
But can your friends tell the difference?

GRAB THESE:

Ready-made pastry
dough, enough for a
9-inch (23 cm) pie

2 cups
(400 g) sugar

2 teaspoons cream
of tartar

36 (600 g)
buttery snack
crackers,
crumbled up

2 cups (240 ml) water

Peel of one
lemon

2 tablespoons
lemon juice

2 tablespoons
margarine or butter

½
teaspoon
ground
cinnamon

9-inch (23 cm)
pie pan

1. **Roll out** half the ready-
made dough, and line the
dish with it. **Scatter**
the crushed crackers
in the pastry shell.

2. **Heat the water**, sugar,
and cream of tartar in a
saucepan. SIMMER for 15
minutes. Add the lemon
peel and lemon juice.

Get an adult to help
with this part.

3. When the syrup cools, pour it over the crushed crackers. Dot the pie filling with butter or margarine.

4. Roll out the rest of the pastry, and cover the pie. Bake the pie for 30 minutes in an oven preheated to 425°F (220°C).

HOW DOES IT WORK?

The **sugar** in this recipe reacts with the cream of tartar (which is an ACID). The reaction produces a strong-flavored chemical, which is similar to one found in apples.

MMmmm

The mixture of sugar and lemon gives our fake apple mixture the sweet, tangy flavor of real apples.

Smelly science

What makes your mouth water?
Usually it is the smell of
something APPETIZING to eat.
Your **nose picks** up the smell
long before you even get it
into your MOUTH.

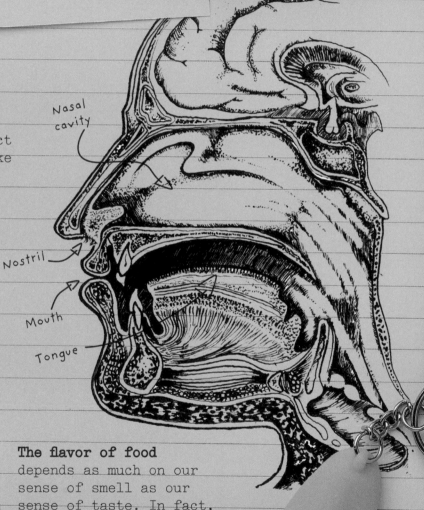

Yummy

The lining of your NASAL CAVITY
(the space behind your nose) is
covered in **thousands** of tiny
sensory cells. These CELLS detect
the different molecules that make
up an odor and **send messages
about the smell to your brain.**
The brain puts the messages
together and you recognize the
smell as being chocolate, or
TOAST, or strawberries.

Nasal cavity

Nostril

Mouth

Tongue

The **tongue** and roof of
the MOUTH are covered
in sensory cells called
taste buds.

The flavor of food
depends as much on our
sense of smell as our
sense of taste. In fact,
we can only detect **five**
tastes with our mouths—
salty, sweet, bitter,
sour, and umami (a
savory flavor). If
you have a BLOCKED
NOSE you can't taste
anything well because
your sense of smell
helps **identify** tastes.

Yuk!

70

IT'S SENSE-SATIONAL!

The **human nose** can detect between 4,000 and 10,000 different smells.

I think it's toffee!

INSECTS CAN DETECT MORE TASTES THAN HUMANS.

They have taste buds on their **feet and antennae** as well as in their mouths.

CERTAIN SMELLS STAY IN OUR MEMORY.
For example, the smell of popcorn can remind you of a trip to the movies or a fairground.

CHILDREN HAVE A BETTER SENSE OF SMELL THAN ADULTS.

They also have **more sensitive** taste buds, but these become less sensitive with age, which is why you like **stronger flavors** (and even vegetables) as you get older.

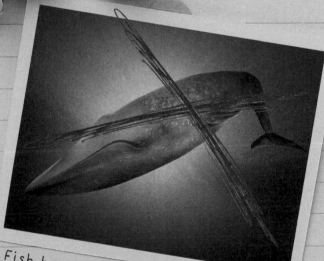

Fish have a keen sense of smell, but **whales and dolphins** and most birds cannot smell ANYTHING.

Many NASTY WHIFFS are caused by chemicals that contain **sulfur.** The most common are hydrogen sulfide (think rotten eggs or **stink bombs**) and thiols. Thiols cause the lovely aromas of garlic, boiled cabbage, and **skunks.**

A dog's nose is 100,000 to 1 MILLION times more sensitive than a human's. **Bloodhounds** are even more sensitive, at 100 million times. They were bred to **track humans** from trails several days old.

Pooh! What a stink!

Soda fountain

This fantastically **messy experiment** blasts a jet of soda high into the air. You'll never look at party food the same way again!

GRAB THESE:

2 pieces of cardboard

A family-size bottle of cola

A roll of mints

Try using different kinds of sodas and candies.

Diet cola works best and is less sticky.

1. **Put the bottle** on the ground outside and take the cap off.

2. **Roll one piece of cardboard** into a tube that fits the neck of the bottle. Unwrap the mints and put them into the tube.

3. **Rest the tube** on the other piece of cardboard, and hold them over the bottleneck.

4. **Pull the cardboard** out, and let all the mints fall into the bottle. Get out of the way—FAST!

HOW DOES IT WORK?

Soda pop contains **carbon dioxide gas** that has been forced into the liquid under pressure. When you unscrew the lid, it releases the pressure and the carbon dioxide forms bubbles. Adding the mints helps the bubbles to escape so quickly that they EXPLODE out of the bottle in a jet of foam.

The surface of each candy is **rough and lumpy**, with lots of tiny hollows that encourage bubbles to attach and grow. As the bubbles EXPAND, the candy rises to the top of the bottle, **releases** the gas, and then sinks again.

When the candies start to **dissolve**, they release gum arabic and gelatin into the liquid. These chemicals help the bubbles to expand and **escape** from the solution.

WHICH COMBINATION OF CANDY AND SODA WORKS BEST?

WARNING

Do this experiment OUTSIDE, since the fountain will spray sticky liquid over a large area. If you have to do it indoors, use the bathroom and a smaller bottle of soda. Make sure you ask your mom first!

Sudden impact

Some things happen so fast that if you blink, you miss them. Even if you don't blink, your brain cannot process the information from your eyes fast enough to see exactly what happened. This is where high-speed photography helps. The camera shutter opens and closes in ONE-MILLIONTH OF A SECOND to capture the instant a bullet smashes through an apple.

As the force of the bullet travels through the apple, the peel splits and the flesh explodes outward. The bullet is traveling at about 500 mph (800 km/h).

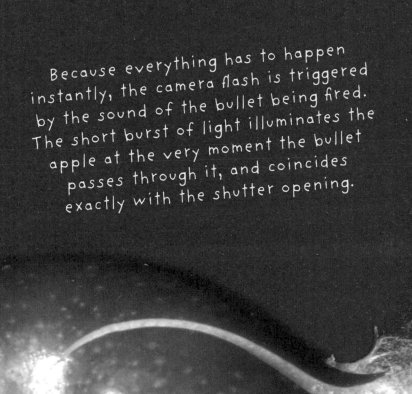

Because everything has to happen instantly, the camera flash is triggered by the sound of the bullet being fired. The short burst of light illuminates the apple at the very moment the bullet passes through it, and coincides exactly with the shutter opening.

When the bullet hits the apple it creates an impact crater. The material at the center of the crater is thrown outward and upward.

Ice cream in a bag

How did people make ice cream before they had freezers? They used the cooling powers of **salt** and **ice**. This recipe makes such good ice cream, you might want to keep it a SECRET, like King Charles I of England. He paid his chef a fortune to keep it under wraps.

Why not add chocolate or banana to your ice cream?

GRAB THESE:

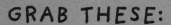
4 tablespoons of salt

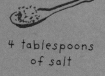
½ cup full-fat milk or cream

4 cups of crushed ice

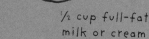
2 small sealable freezer bags

1 tablespoon sugar

A towel or warm gloves

1 large sealable bag

½ teaspoon vanilla flavoring

1. **Pour the milk**, sugar, and vanilla into a small bag. (Or mix them in a pitcher first.) Zip up the bag, making sure there is not too much AIR left inside. Put this inside the other small bag, again **squeezing** out the air, and zip it up.

HOW DOES IT WORK?

When ice melts it **takes in energy** in the form of heat from the surrounding environment.

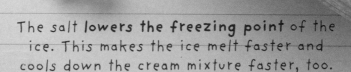

The water in the milk freezes and forms ICE CRYSTALS.

In this experiment, the melting ice takes heat from the **ingredients** of the ice cream, making them colder.

The salt **lowers the freezing point** of the ice. This makes the ice melt faster and cools down the cream mixture faster, too.

(2.) **Put the crushed ice** into the large bag and sprinkle it with the salt. Put the smaller bags in the middle of the ice. Squeeze as much air as possible out of the big bag and seal it. Removing the air from the bags stops them POPPING open when they are shaken.

(3.) **Wrap the bag in the towel** or put your gloves on. Shake and **squish** the bag, making sure the ice surrounds the ice-cream mixture. It should take about 5 to 10 minutes for the mixture to freeze.

What else can you freeze like this? You could try fruit juice.

Chilling out

Sometimes the best discoveries are made by mistake. In 1905, 11-year-old Frank Epperson left a fruit-flavored soda drink on his porch during a cold night. When he came back to it, the stirring stick had frozen to the drink. He had invented the **ice pop!**

Ever wondered why some ice pops are soft while others are ROCK HARD? It all depends on how much sugar the ice pop contains. Sugary liquids melt at a much lower temperature than water. So a sugary ice pop is always softer than a watery one if they are at the same temperature.

An ice pop is about 90 percent water.

Ice melts as it is warmed up by the air.

Why would anyone live in a house made of ice? Ice doesn't carry heat well—it's a very good insulator. So body heat doesn't escape from the inside of an igloo.

Have you ever had brain freeze? About 40 percent of people get sudden **headaches** when they eat icy foods too fast. But scientists don't know exactly why this happens.

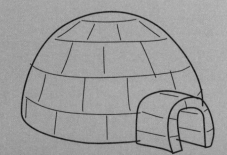

Ice pops melt at about 30°F (-1°C).

In 2005, a beverage company tried to erect a 25-ft (7.5 m) tall ice pop in New York City's Union Square. It **melted faster** than anyone expected, and onlookers had to flee from a FLOOD of kiwi and strawberry flavored gloop.

Ice pops aren't always this messy! A Danish company has invented an ice pop that doesn't drip. Instead of turning to liquid, it turns to **jelly**.

Water molecules in ice lock together in hexagonal crystals.

Have you ever gotten your tongue STUCK to an ice pop? This happens when the moisture on your tongue freezes. **Ouch!**

Why is ice so slippery?

Ice melts more easily when pressure is put on it. This makes it slippery.

TURN UP THE VOLUME

Kaboom! This Tomcat fighter jet has just smashed through the speed of sound, leaving a **sonic boom cloud** behind it. This section is full of noisy science. You can rock out with homemade instruments, discover how people "see" the world with echoes, and check out the world's NOISIEST animal.

Recycled rock band

Have you ever heard musicians talking about "good vibes"? "Vibes" is short for VIBRATIONS, which is what all sound, including music, is made up of. Different instruments make different vibrations in the air. Here's how you can make some vibes of your own, by **building your own band!**

1. Using a pitcher or funnel, pour different amounts of water into the glass jars or bottles.

Mark the water levels of notes you like with tape.

BLOW YOUR OWN TRUMPET

GRAB THESE:

Length of tubing or pipe

Modeling clay—for smoothing rough edges and filling in any gaps between the mouthpiece and the tube

A plastic bottle

1. **Make a mouthpiece** by cutting the top off a plastic bottle. Ideally this should be about 1 in (25 mm) below the bottom of the screw thread where the bottle begins to flare out.

2. **Stick the narrow end** of your mouthpiece into the opening of a piece of tubing. Put your mouth against the mouthpiece. Purse your lips together and blow through them to create a BUZZ. Try this with different containers, such as bottles or a watering can, to see what sounds they make.

HOW DOES IT WORK?

BUZZING into the mouthpiece makes the air in the tube vibrate. The sound waves **bounce off the sides** of the tube to produce a sound with a particular pitch. You can change the pitch by slackening or tightening your lips.

BOTTLE PIANO

The bottles vibrate to create a sound.

DING
DING

2. Tap each bottle with a spoon. If you want a HIGHER note, pour some of the water out. If you want a **lower** note, add more water. The more bottles you have, the more notes you can produce.

Add food coloring to make it look good.

GRAB THESE:

Glass bottles or jars, preferably all the same size

Pitcher   Food coloring

Tape

Spoon

JUNGLE DRUMS

GRAB THESE:

Empty bowls or cans

Thick plastic bags

Chopsticks

Strong rubber bands

Tape

The plastic vibrates when it's hit, which makes the air vibrate, too.

1. Cut out a square of plastic that's at least 2 in (5 cm) wider than the the bowl or can. Put it over the opening of the bowl, STRETCHING it as tightly as possible. Secure it with a rubber band.

Instead of producing a pure note, most drums simply produce a NOISE, but some drums can be tuned to a particular pitch.

2. Attach the edge of the plastic to the container with tape. You can then use chopsticks or spoons to beat out a rhythm. Don't bang too hard!

What is sound?

When you play an instrument (or talk, or sing, or even belch) you are creating sound. Sound is a form of ENERGY. Like many other forms of energy, it travels in **waves**.

When a tight string is plucked it starts to ViBRaTe. As the string moves to one side, it pushes the AIR MOLECULES next to it together. Then, as the string moves back in the opposite direction it **creates a gap**. This alternating system of pushing molecules together and creating a gap is called a COMPRESSION WAVE.

When you play an instrument you set something VIBRATING, either by BASHING it, BLOWING down it, PLUCKING it, or SCRAPING it.

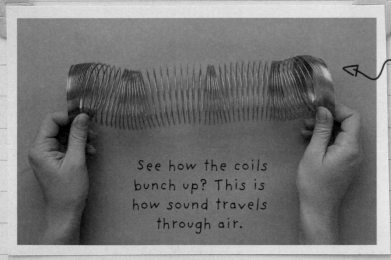

See how the coils bunch up? This is how sound travels through air.

You can see how compression waves work if two people hold either end of a Slinky toy. If one person PINCHES a number of coils together at their end and then **lets go**, you can see that the group of coils travel CLOSE TOGETHER until they reach the other end.

The shape of the wave tells you the sound's pitch (high or low) and how loud it is. High notes produce waves with **peaks and troughs** that are close together. Low notes have peaks and troughs that are FARTHER APART. Loud sounds produce tall waves, soft sounds are much **flatter**.

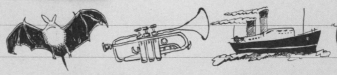

High & soft

High & loud

Low & loud

Low & soft

SOUND FACTS

It's no use shouting for help in outer space—no one can hear you. Sound needs something to travel through, but in space there's no air, so it's completely silent.

The loudest sound ever to have been heard may have been that of the **asteroid** that smashed into Earth 65 million years ago and triggered the extinction of ⟶ the dinosaurs.

Hello... can you hear me?

We measure sound in decibels. The space shuttle generates more than 200 decibels at launch. The noise is so loud **it can be fatal** at close range.

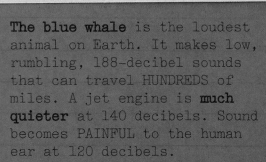

Aargh! My ears!!!

The blue whale is the loudest animal on Earth. It makes low, rumbling, 188-decibel sounds that can travel HUNDREDS of miles. A jet engine is **much quieter** at 140 decibels. Sound becomes PAINFUL to the human ear at 120 decibels.

Human ears cannot hear every sound. This is GOOD, otherwise the world would be **too noisy** for us to cope with.

THE BLAST LAB BUGLE

Issue Number 987,654,321

READ ALL ABOUT IT! READ ALL ABOUT IT!

MUSIC-CRAZY BAT CRASHES INTO TREE

Brian Flap had been listening to Batney Spears on his new MP3 player at the time of the accident. Shortly before hitting the tree, he narrowly avoided an owl in midair. The startled bird called out, "Hey! Listen where you're going!"

EXCLUSIVE

HEARING IS BELIEVING

Most bats depend on their sense of hearing to "see" where they're going. They make high-pitched clicks, and listen for the echoes. They can then tell where objects are depending on how soon they hear echoes in each ear. This is called echolocation. Dolphins and some whales also use echolocation to find shoals of fish.

AMAZING BUT TRUE

HUMAN "BATS"

SOME PEOPLE CAN SEE WITH THEIR EARS

Some blind people have learned to use echolocation. They can build a picture of the world around them by tapping a cane or clicking their tongue, and listening to the echoes. Instructor Daniel Kish teaches blind people to hike and even cycle using echolocation.

where's that sound?

We use **both ears** together to figure out where NOISES come from.

If a sound is louder in your **left ear**, you know that the thing making that sound is to your LEFT. It's the same for your right ear.

Ignore me—I'm just hanging around.

Ooo-eee, this way!

BANG BANG!

Hey, over here!

WHAT HAPPENS IF SOUNDS TRAVEL TO THE WRONG EAR?

Here's an experiment that messes with your **hearing**. Connect two funnels to flexible **tubes** and attach them so the tubes cross. Get a friend to wear this HEADSET with the tubes in their ears and their eyes closed. Then make noises from different parts of the room.

Can **your friend tell** where the noises are coming from?

Homemade headphones

Don't **throw away** those old, broken headphones. Here's a way you can recycle them into a snazzy NEW pair that **really work**. Plug them into a computer or MP3 player, and get ready to rock!

GRAB THESE:

Old or broken headphones

2 paper cups

Cardboard

2 lengths of wire about 10 ft (3 m) long

4 small neodymium magnets (from a hardware store)

Scissors

A candle

Tape

A hairband

HOW TO MAKE A SPEAKER

①. **Cut out a rectangle** of cardboard 3 in x 4 in (8 cm x 10 cm). Roll this into a tube, and tape it closed. Then cut out a circle of cardboard. Use tape to attach the circle to the tube.

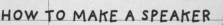

It will be easier to tape things to the tube if you make little cuts at either end.

THE MORE COILS IN THE WIRE, THE LOUDER YOUR SPEAKER WILL BE.

②. **Stack two magnets** together and tape them securely to the bottom of the cup. Then put the cardboard tube over the magnets and **tape it to the cup.**

HOW TO CONNECT THE SPEAKERS

5. Cut an ear bud off the old headphones. This should reveal **two wires**. Ask an adult to strip back the plastic and to hold the two wires in a candle flame for a few seconds to expose the metal. Twist each wire onto one of the wires from the speaker, and fix it in place with tape.

Repeat for the other speaker.

You can join your headphones together by cutting a slot in the rim of each cup and pushing them on to the hairband.

HOW DOES IT WORK?

When a flow of electricity is sent around a coiled wire (like the one in our speakers) it creates a **magnetic field**, with a north and south pole. This flow keeps changing direction. Each time it changes, the poles of the magnetic field **swap over**.

Every time the wire's magnetic field changes, the magnets on the cup move in a different direction. They PUSH AND PULL the bottom of the cup, creating **vibrations** in the air. These vibrations are SOUND WAVES.

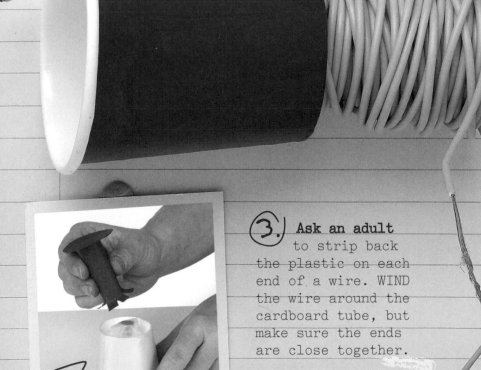

Cut

3. **Ask an adult** to strip back the plastic on each end of a wire. WIND the wire around the cardboard tube, but make sure the ends are close together.

4. **To make the second speaker,** go back to the first step and repeat. When you've made **both,** you can connect them together: see the top of this page.

89

Blow that horn!

Brass instruments like this mini trumpet are really just long tubes. They work by trapping a mixture of sound waves and magnifying some of them. A long tube magnifies long waves (which sound deep) and a short tube magnifies short waves (which sound high).

When these buttons are pressed down, they change the length of the tube. This increases the number of notes the musician can play.

Mouthpiece

Tube

A trumpet player makes a sort of buzzing sound into the mouthpiece. By making tiny changes to the shape of his mouth, he alters the sound that comes out of the bell.

The tube is coiled up so the trumpet is compact and easy to hold.

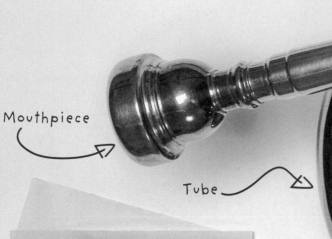

Brass instruments make a lot of NOISE!

Brass instruments aren't always made of brass—they can be made of other metals, wood, or shell.

Bell

Sound comes out here. When the musician covers the bell of the trumpet, the sound is softer and quieter.

Trumpet players produce a lot of spit. This clogs up the instrument and makes it sound gurgly, so the player opens a special valve, called a spit valve, to let it dribble out. Eww!

Spit

Valve

The trumpet was invented in China around 2000 BCE. It was straight, and was used for sending out signals.

Glossary

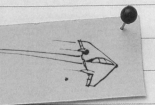

Acid
A sharp or sour-tasting chemical. Vinegar and lemon juice are both acids.

Aerodynamics
The science of how objects move through the air.

Air pressure
A pushing or squeezing force caused by the air.

Antenna (feeler)
A sense organ on an insect's head, used for touching and tasting things.

Argon
A gas found in Earth's atmosphere, which doesn't react with other chemicals.

Asteroid
A rocky object smaller than a planet, traveling in an orbit around the Sun.

Atmosphere
The layer of air around Earth.

Atom
A minute particle of matter that cannot be divided (except in a nuclear explosion).

Bacteria
Single-celled microscopic organisms that can cause diseases in humans.

Base
A chemical that reacts with acids, also called an alkali. Baking soda is one kind of base.

Battery
A device used to store electrical energy.

Carbon dioxide
A gas made of carbon and oxygen atoms.

Circuit
The path through which electricity flows when an electrical device is switched on.

Crystal
A solid whose atoms or molecules are lined up in a regular pattern.

Decibel
A measurement of how loud a sound is.

Digestion
The process of breaking food down into chemicals that can be used by the body.

Drag
A force that holds back objects when they move through air or water. Drag is caused by air or water molecules getting in the way.

Echolocation
The detection of objects using sound rather than sight.

Electricity
A form of energy that can be transmitted by wires.

Electromagnet
A type of magnet in which the magnetic field is produced by electricity.

Electron
A particle with a negative charge that orbits the nucleus of an atom.

Energy
The capacity to make some kind of action happen.

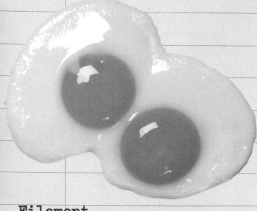

Filament
A thin, flexible thread, such as the delicate wire inside a light bulb that glows when the light is switched on.

Fluid
A substance such as a liquid or gas that can move freely and does not have a fixed shape.

Force
A push or a pull.

Freezing point
The temperature at which water turns to ice.

Gelatin
A jellylike material used in cooking.

Germs
Tiny organisms, smaller than the eye can see, that cause illnesses.

Gum arabic
A tough, chewy sap produced by African trees. It's used for making chewing gum, candy, and glue.

Helium
A gas that is lighter than air. A balloon filled with helium will float.

Hydrogen sulfide
The gas that gives rotten eggs their unpleasant smell. It is poisonous in large amounts.

Impact
Sudden, powerful collision, such as when two objects hit each other.

Insulator
A substance that doesn't easily allow energy to pass through it. Different kinds of insulators resist heat, electricity, and sound.

Interference
A pattern of waves caused by two or more sets of waves colliding together.

Lift
An upward force, generated by a wing, that keeps flying objects in the air.

Magnet
An object that can pull iron or certain other types of metal without touching them.

Mass
The amount of matter in an object.

Microwave
A kind of energy that is used to heat food in microwave ovens.

Molecule
A tiny unit of matter, made of two or more atoms bonded together.

Non-Newtonian fluid
A soft substance that becomes either runnier or thicker when squeezed or pushed.

Potential energy
A form of stored energy that can be turned into another type of energy.

Pressure
The effect of a force pushing against an object.

Protein
A type of organic molecule found in animals and plants.

Reaction
When the bonds that hold chemicals together are broken, and they change into different chemicals.

Sensory cells
Special cells that create senses such as smell, taste, vision, touch, and pain.

Solution
A substance completely dissolved in another substance.

Glossary

Sonic boom
The deafening boom made by an aircraft traveling faster than the speed of sound.

Spectrum
The range of colors produced when white light is split by a prism, such as a raindrop.

Surface tension
The effect that makes water seem to have an elastic skin. It is caused by the strong attraction of the molecules on the surface of a liquid.

Taste buds
Sensory cells on the tongue and inside the mouth that detect different types of flavors.

Terminal
The part of a battery that wires are connected to. There are two terminals on a battery: the negative and positive terminals.

Terminal velocity
The maximum speed an object reaches when falling to Earth.

Thrust
A pushing force.

Ultraviolet
A color that humans cannot normally see, but which is visible to bees and some other insects.

Vacuum
An empty space from which all the air molecules have been removed.

Vibration
The rapid back and forth movement of an object, such as a plucked guitar string.

Wave
An up-and-down pattern that forms when energy travels through air, water, or some other medium.

Index

Acknowledgments

Dorling Kindersley would like to thank the following people and organizations for help with this book: Lisa Magloff, Lorrie Mack, Alexander Cox, and Easter Parade.

The publisher would like to thank the following for their kind permission to reproduce their photographs:

(Key: a-above; b-below/bottom; c-center; f-far; l-left; r-right; t-top)

Alamy Images: Andi Duff 44bc; Dennis Fast/Vwpics/Visual&Written SL 34bl; Tony Harrington/StockShot 55cla; A. T. Willett 80-81; Worldspec/NASA 12, 85c. **Corbis:** Heide Benser/Zefa 39br; Bettmann 55crb; John and Lisa Merrill 30cr; Rudy Sulgan 31cr. **DK Images:** Natural History Museum, London 22tr. **Flickr.com:** MRHSfan/Melissa Jones 73. **Fortean Picture Library:** Werner Burger 35clb. **fotolia:** Orkhan Aslanov 63.

Getty Images: Photographer's Choice/Images Etc Ltd 28-29; Science Faction/Charles Krebs 22-23; Science Faction/William Radcliffe 50l. **iStockphoto.com:** BMPix 58br; Lim Beng Chee 45bl, 45ca (egg), 45cr, 45fcrb (egg), 92fcra (egg); Jill Chen 72bl; Deborah Cheramie 71bc; Palto 45ca (parachute), 45cl, 45fcr (parachute), 45tr, 92fcra (parachute); Bela Tibor Kozma 70bl; Vinicius Ramalho Tupinamba 44cra. **Thomas Marent:** 36-37. **naturepl.com:** Doc White 85cr. **Rex Features:** Sipa Press 8-9. **Science Photo Library:** Eye Of Science 59; Michael Giannechini 35tr; Edward Kinsman 74-75, 94r; Lawrence Lawry 2; Pekka Parviainen 35cla; Volker Steger 40-41; Sheila Terry 13clb; Victor Habbick Visions 86clb; Kent Wood 50-51. **SeaPics.com:** Phillip Colla 71cr. **September Films 2008 Photographs by Alex Maguire:** 2-3, 94-95.

All other images © Dorling Kindersley
For further information see: **www.dkimages.com**